DRAW SCIENCE

Dinosaurs

By Nina Kidd

Lowell House
Juvenile
Los Angeles

Contemporary Books
Chicago

To Scott, a dinosaur lover

Reviewed and endorsed by Q. L. Pearce, author of *All About Dinosaurs, Tyrannosaurus Rex and Other Dinosaur Wonders,* and *How to Talk Dinosaur with Your Child*

Requests for such permissions should be addressed to:
Lowell House Juvenile
2029 Century Park East, Suite 3290
Los Angeles, CA 90067

Publisher: Jack Artenstein
Executive Vice-President: Nick Clemente
Editor-in-Chief: Lisa Melton

Manufactured in the United States of America.

ISBN: 0-929923-89-8

10 9 8 7 6 5 4 3 2 1

CONTENTS

Drawing Tips

This book shows you how to draw 24 different dinosaurs. There are lots of different ways to draw, and here are just a few. You'll find some helpful hints throughout this book to help make your drawings the best they can be.

Before you begin, here are some tips that every aspiring artist should know!

- Use a large sheet of paper, and make your drawing fill up the space. It's easier to see what you are doing, and you will have plenty of room to add details.

- When you are blocking in the large shapes, draw by moving your whole arm, not just your fingers.

- Experiment with different kinds of lines: do a light line, then gradually bear down for a wider, darker one. Try groups of lines: straight, crossing, curved, jagged. You'll find that just by changing the thickness of a line, your whole picture will look different!

- Remember every artist has his or her own style. Your picture shouldn't look exactly like the one in the book. It should reflect your own creativity.

- Most of all, have fun!

What You'll Need

PAPER

Many kinds of paper can be used, but some are better than others. For pencil drawing, avoid newsprint or rough papers because they don't erase well. Instead, use a large pad of bond paper (or a similar type of paper). The paper doesn't have to be thick, but it should be uncoated, smooth, and cold pressed. You can find bond paper at an art store. If you are using ink, a dull-finished, coated paper works best.

PENCILS, CHARCOAL, AND PENS

A regular school pencil is fine for drawing, but try to use one with a soft lead. Pencils with soft lead are labeled #2; #3 pencils have a hard lead. If you want a thicker lead, ask an art store clerk or an art teacher for an artist's drafting pencil.

Charcoal will give you a very black line, but it smudges easily and is hard to control in small drawings. If you want to use charcoal, start with a charcoal pencil of medium to hard grade. With it, you will be able to rub in shadows, then erase certain areas to make highlights.

If you want a smooth, thin ink line, try a rolling-point or a fiber-point pen. Art stores and larger stationery stores have them in a variety of line widths and fun, bright colors.

ERASERS

An eraser is one of your most important tools! Besides removing unwanted lines and cleaning up smudges, erasers can be used to make highlights and textures. Get a soft plastic type (the white ones are good), or for very small areas, a gray kneaded eraser can be useful. Try not to take off ink with an eraser because it will ruin the drawing paper. If you must take an ink line out of your picture, use liquid whiteout.

OTHER HANDY TOOLS

Facial tissues are helpful for creating soft shadows—just go over your pencil marks with a tissue and rub it gently around the area you want smoothed out.

A square of metal window screen is another tool that can be used to make shadows. Hold it just above your paper and rub a soft pencil lead on it. Then rub the shavings from the pencil into the paper to make a smooth shadowed area in your picture. If you like, you can add a sharp edge to the shadow with your eraser.

You will also need a pencil sharpener, but if you don't have one, rub the side of your pencil point against a small piece of sandpaper to keep the point sharp.

Backgrounds

Once you have completed a drawing, you may want to put your animal in a setting. An encyclopedia or some travel guides will show you what the plants and land look like where the animal lived. Or, use your imagination! Here are some suggestions for different settings.

MAGAZINE BACKGROUNDS

If you like to cut and paste, ask your family for some old magazines you can cut up. If your animal lived on the plains, cut out distant volcanoes with wispy smoke. Or cut out different patterns and cut them into the shapes of volcanoes and smoke! This will give your picture an abstract, funky look. And you don't have to fill the entire page— just a few trees or some mountains in the background will give the impression of a whole scene.

PAINTED BACKGROUNDS

You don't need a paintbrush to add *these* painted backgrounds! If you want to make an animal's footprints, dip the round end of a pencil eraser into some paint and print it on your drawing in groupings of four or five.

For other shapes and textures, also try cut edges of corrugated board, an old toothbrush, the end of an old spool, or a cut piece of Styrofoam. Also try using crumpled wax paper or a paper towel. Be sure not to get them too wet or they won't work well.

TEXTURED BACKGROUNDS

If you want to create a textured background, you'll need to draw your animal on a thin piece of paper. Grab a pencil with a thick lead and place a textured object (such as a thick-veined leaf) under the section of your paper where you want the texture to appear. Then rub evenly and lightly over the area with the side of your pencil lead. Try sandpaper, window screening, rough wood, pavement, a fine kitchen grater—anything you can imagine!

SHADOWED BACKGROUNDS

By adding shadows in just the right places, your prehistoric animals will leap off the page! Imagine where the shadow of your animal would fall underneath its tail, neck, and belly. Then fill in those places with dark pencil. If you need some help figuring out where a shadow might fall, experiment with your own shadow! Go outside and see where it falls during different times of the day. Notice, too, how long your shadow is. Depending on the time of day, a shadow may shrink or grow. If you wanted your animal to cast a morning shadow, the shadow would be very long. How would that shadow look at noon?

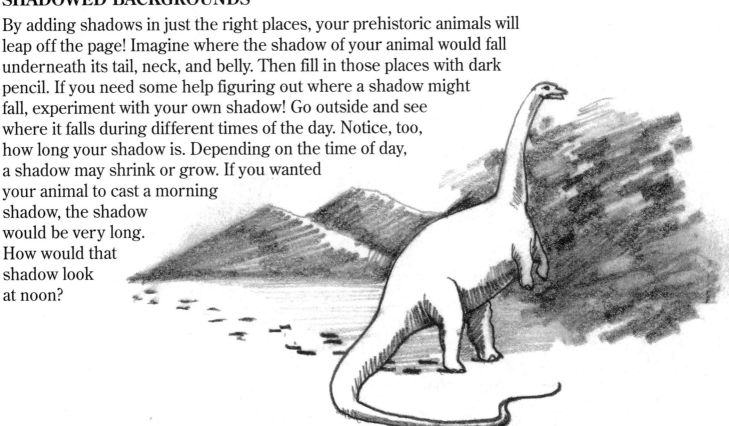

Finishing Your Drawing

Artists use many finishing techniques to make their animals seem real. Here are some very useful techniques for giving your drawings a natural look. As you'll see with the example of *Chasmosaurus*, different techniques result in very different looks.

HATCHING

Hatching is a group of short, straight lines used to create a texture or a shadow. When you curve the hatching lines, you create a rounded look. This is handy when texturing an animal's legs, neck, or underside, as shown on *Chasmosaurus*. When you draw the hatching lines close together, you create a dark shadow, such as with the right hindleg and underside of the tail. For very light shading, draw the lines shorter, thinner, and farther apart, as shown on *Chasmosaurus's* face and forelegs.

CROSS-HATCHING

This technique gives your animal a wrinkled look. Start with an area of hatching, then crisscross it with a new set of lines. If you are drawing wrinkles on skin, make the lines a bit wobbly and uneven, just as creases in real skin would be. Take a look at *Chasmosaurus's* frill to see how larger cross-hatching works well for big areas of skin, while smaller cross-hatching looks good in smaller areas, such as on the animal's chest.

STIPPLE

When you want to give your drawing a different feel, try the stipple technique—and all you need are dots! This method works best with a pen, because unlike a pencil, a pen will make an even black dot by just touching the paper. You can make a shadow almost black just by placing the dots closer together. The stipple technique is very similar to the way photos are printed in newspapers and books. If you look through a magnifying glass at a picture in a newspaper, you will see very tiny dots. Note that they are small and far apart in the light areas, and larger and closer to each other in the dark areas.

SMOOTH TONE

By using the side of your pencil, you can create a smooth texture on your creature. Start in the lighter areas with the side of the pencil, stroking very lightly and evenly. Put a little bit more pressure on your pencil as you move to the areas you want to be darker. If you want something even smoother, go back and rub the pencil with a facial tissue, but rub gently! If you get smudges in areas you want to stay white, simply remove them with an eraser.

SPECIALIZED SKIN TEXTURES

In this drawing, *Chasmosaurus* has squarish shapes to suggest scales. Notice how the squares get smaller on the leg and face and seem to curve around its legs and back. On its underside the lines are thicker to suggest a shadow. You can also combine the squarish shapes with stippling to create a pattern of rough, dense scales for *Chasmosaurus*.

Now that you're armed with the basic drawing tools and techniques, you're ready to get started on the dinosaurs and other prehistoric creatures in this book. What's more, you'll learn as you draw! After each drawing step, you'll find some scientific information that is not only fun and interesting to know, but is also useful when it comes to drawing.

Throughout the book, too, you'll find special Drawing Tips that will aid your progress. Last, at the back of the book are extra techniques and hints for using color, casting shadows, placing animals in a scene—in short, making the most of your drawings.

Dimetrodon was a member of a group of mammal-like reptiles (the pelycosaurs) that lived around 280 million years ago,

① Begin this interesting reptile by drawing a long oval for its body.

Dimetrodon's *low-slung body averaged about 10 feet in length.*

② Next draw a five-sided shape for the head as shown. Then draw a large line from the head and create a big hump over the back for the huge sail fin. Extend the line straight out past the body for the tail. Add two circular shapes for the thick upper legs.

Dimetrodon's *back sail fin was supported by long, bony spines that extended from the backbone. The longest spine stood about three feet high.*

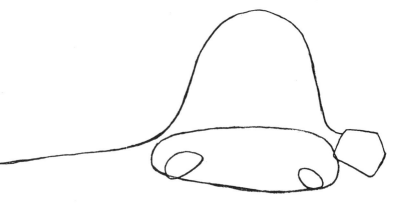

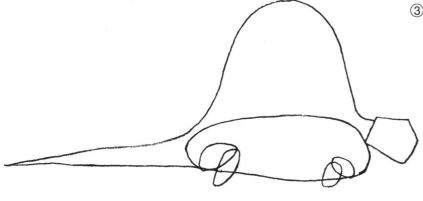

③ Indicate the underside of the tail with a line. Then sketch the lower sections of the legs.

Scientists believe the back sail fin was covered with skin well supplied with blood vessels. On a clear day, with the sunlight streaming on its fin, Dimetrodon could probably warm up and begin hunting in less than half the time it took another reptile of the same size to wake and move about.

MORE SCIENCE: *Dimetrodon* was a member of a large class of animals called synapsids. The synapsids eventually produced the therapsids, which were the direct ancestors of mammals.

well before the age of the dinosaurs. *Dimetrodon* in Greek means "two kinds of teeth."

④ Now pencil in the eye and the eye ridge, as well as a wavy shape for the mouth. Add a lower neckline and three feet.

Remains of this unusual animal have been found in the states of Oklahoma and Texas. Two dinosaurs with temperature-regulating sail fins on their backs have been discovered in Africa, but they are unrelated to Dimetrodon.

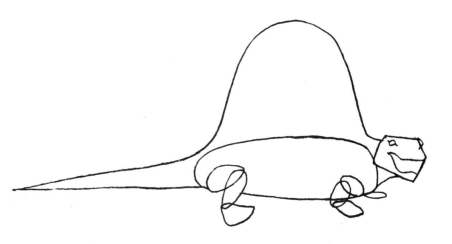

⑤ Draw the supporting spines for the sail fin. Pencil in nostrils, sharp teeth, toes, and claws. Erase all unnecessary joint lines around the face, neck, feet, and tail.

Like today's mammals, including humans, Dimetrodon *had more than one kind of teeth. With its large canines and other cutting teeth, it could capture and slice up its food more effectively than other reptiles not so equipped.*

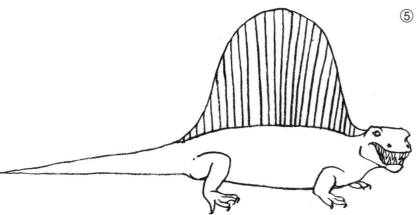

⑥ Shade in the skin and sail membrane with hatching, using varying lengths of strokes. Fill in the mouth and eye. Watch out—*Dimetrodon* is ready to crawl away!

It's easy to see that Dimetrodon *wasn't a dinosaur by its sprawling stance. Dinosaurs stood more erect, with their legs beneath their bodies rather than to the side.*

Mesosaurus

was not a dinosaur, but a swimming reptile that was very small. Despite its fierce-looking jaws, it probably

① To begin *Mesosaurus*, draw a curved zigzag line, which runs from the tip of the creature's tail to the base of its head. Add a thin oval for the body in the lower section of the long, curving line.

   Mesosaurus's *tail was long and flat with top and bottom fins, making it a strong swimmer.*

② Then draw a circle at the bottom of the line for the base of *Mesosaurus's* head. Sketch in the four legs.

   Mesosaurus *was just over a yard long.*

③ Now add the outlines for the four webbed feet. Begin to add dimension by drawing several curved lines in the tail.

   Mesosaurus's *webbed front and back feet helped it swim efficiently. The back legs worked with the tail to create forward motion, while the front legs were used to steer.*

MORE SCIENCE: *Mesosaurus* lived about 280 million years ago—long before the dinosaurs.

lived on tiny sea creatures, which it strained through its fine teeth.

④ Draw a rectangular guideline for the jaws. Complete the neck by adding a lower line from the head to the body.

Mesosaurus's needlelike teeth probably worked like filters. After taking a large gulp of water, excess water would be forced out between the teeth while small aquatic animals remained in its mouth.

⑤ Next insert a V shape for the narrow jaws. Add an eye circle. Indicate the webbing between the toes. Erase all unnecessary lines—don't forget to erase a small section of the curved line on *Mesosaurus's* back.

Nostrils and eyes high on the snout allowed Mesosaurus *to breathe air and see above water while it was almost completely submerged.*

⑥ Use dark, spiky lines to detail the teeth and the ribs along the tail fin. Add stipple throughout for skin texture, concentrating more on the face and tail. Last, fill in the eye and watch *Mesosaurus* swim away!

Remains of Mesosaurus *have been found in southern Africa and South America.*

DRAWING TIP: When drawing your *Mesosaurus*, it will be helpful to think of its feet as being alligator feet, and the body and tail fins as being similar to those of a modern fish.

Longisquama

was one of the smallest prehistoric reptiles. It was also among the most dramatic in appearance. But as

① First draw a narrow oval for the body of *Longisquama*.

In existence about 240 million years ago, Longisquama *was one of a large group of reptiles called "thecodonts," whose descendants included the dinosaurs, the flying pterosaurs, and the modern crocodile.*

② Next sketch in a triangular head. Extend the tail line past the body in a slight arc. Draw the three visible upper leg sections.

Longisquama *was only six inches long and probably preyed on insects.*

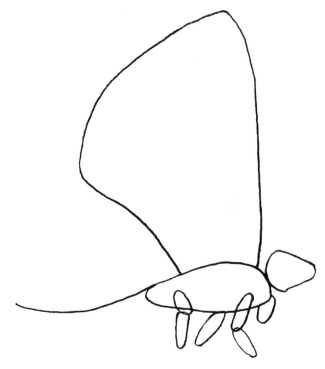

③ Now draw the outline that will hold the creature's spikes. Indicate three of the lower legs.

Remains of Longisquama *have been found in southwest Asia.*

MORE SCIENCE: Some paleontologists think that *Longisquama's* upright spines could have been the beginning of the development of feathers.

far as we know, the flaired spiky formations on its back did not serve any obvious purpose.

④ Add the fourth lower leg and sketch in the feet.

This early reptile's spines could have been used for display to attract mates or for help in gliding through the air. Their real purpose is unknown.

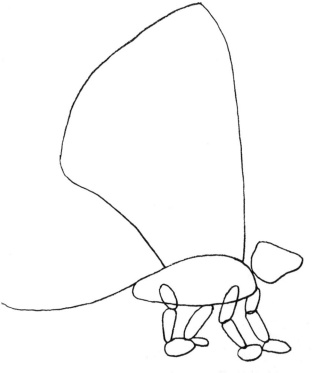

⑤ Define the toes, the claws, the eye, and the long, narrow spines. Add an open mouth. Sketch a small, ragged edge at the base of the tail. Erase all unnecessary overlapping lines.

Looking somewhat like a lizard, Longisquama's *body scales had ridges running from front to rear.*

⑥ Use cross-hatching to give the legs texture. Sketch small V marks on its back and around its head. Shade the spikes with diagonal lines. If *Longisquama's* spines were for display, they might have been very brightly colored. Choose your own color when you draw them.

Longisquama *was a very unusual animal. Thus far, scientists have not been able to determine in which thecodont family it belongs.*

Kannemeyeria

was one of a group of mammal-like reptiles, the dicynodonts, that originated before the dinosaurs developed. Dicynodonts' mouth structure

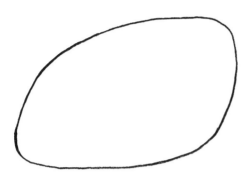

① Begin your *Kannemeyeria* by drawing a rounded, irregular shape for the body.

The large skull of this plant eater was quite light due to large openings for the eyes and nostrils.

② Next draw an oval for the crest, which will sit on the back of this creature's head. Add two upper leg shapes. Extend the tail line down past the body.

The stubby tail probably wasn't used for balance by this low-lying, stocky animal, who most likely lived on forested land.

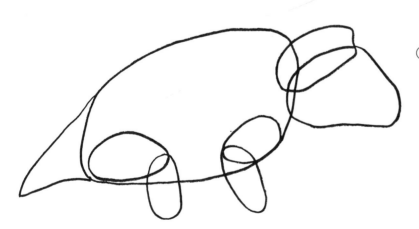

③ Sketch in a large muzzle shape, which should overlap the crest. Add the visible lower legs. Then draw in the underside of the tail.

Kannemeyeria's very strong jaws helped it to eat efficiently. As a group, the dicynodonts survived almost 50 million years.

MORE SCIENCE: Remains of this reptile have been found in Asia, Africa, and South America. *Kannemeyeria* lived about 240 million years ago.

included a plant-clipping beak. A pair of doglike tusks protruded from the upper jaw. *Kannemeyeria* was about 10 feet long, the length of a small car.

④ Next add the four clawed feet. Draw connecting lines from the muzzle and the crest to the body.

Most relatives of this reptile were smaller than Kannemeyeria. *Some lived as modern hippos do, foraging for water plants; others probably dug in the earth for roots. They all had characteristic pairs of canine teeth.*

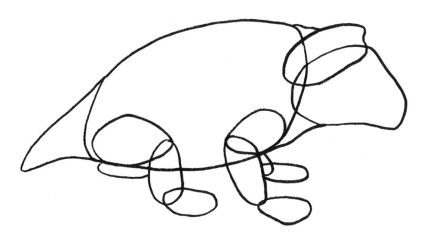

⑤ Pencil in the details on *Kannemeyeria's* head: an eye, a nostril, an ear opening, a beak tip, and one protruding, pointed tooth. Add the toes and claws on each foot as shown. Begin adding detail by indicating crease lines in the reptile's neck. Erase all unnecessary lines to create a smooth body outline.

Kannemeyeria's *beak was made of a hornlike material. The animal could snip off large mouthfuls of roots or leafy branches and grind them down with the toothless edges of its beak.*

⑥ Outline the camouflage skin pattern and fill it in with dark, heavy shading. Color in the eye and the nostril, and shade the face with smaller spots. Don't forget to add highlights to the claws to show how sharp they are!

Kannemeyeria's *skin was probably similar in texture to today's rhinoceros. A heavily built animal, it was probably rather slow and clumsy, but strong.*

DRAWING TIP: If you took away its crest and the tusklike projections for its upper jaw, *Kannemeyeria's* face would look very similar to that of a modern tortoise.

Oviraptor was a toothless dinosaur that stood about chest high to a

① First draw a slightly bent pear shape for *Oviraptor's* body.

Oviraptor *lived in the late Cretaceous period, about 70 million years ago.*

② Next draw a small head shape and connect it to the body with a curved neckline. To the rear, add a long, wavy tail line. Sketch in the large upper hindleg.

Oviraptor's *head was unusually stubby and deep, like a puffin or parrot. Its crested beak had no teeth, but it had muscle attachments that made it strong enough to crush bones.*

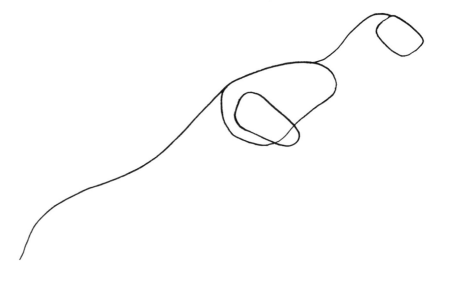

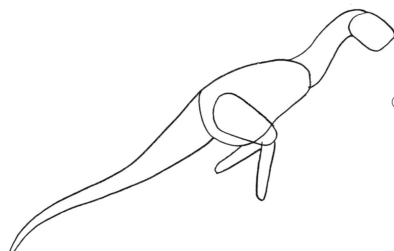

③ Now draw lines for the undersides of the neck and tail. Add two lower leg sections. As you may be able to tell, *Oviraptor* walked on two legs rather than four.

Running on long legs, Oviraptor *used its flexible tail to help it balance.*

MORE SCIENCE: Some members of the *Oviraptor* family may have lived along the shores of inland lakes and may have used their powerful jaws to crack shellfish.

man. Its name means "egg thief."

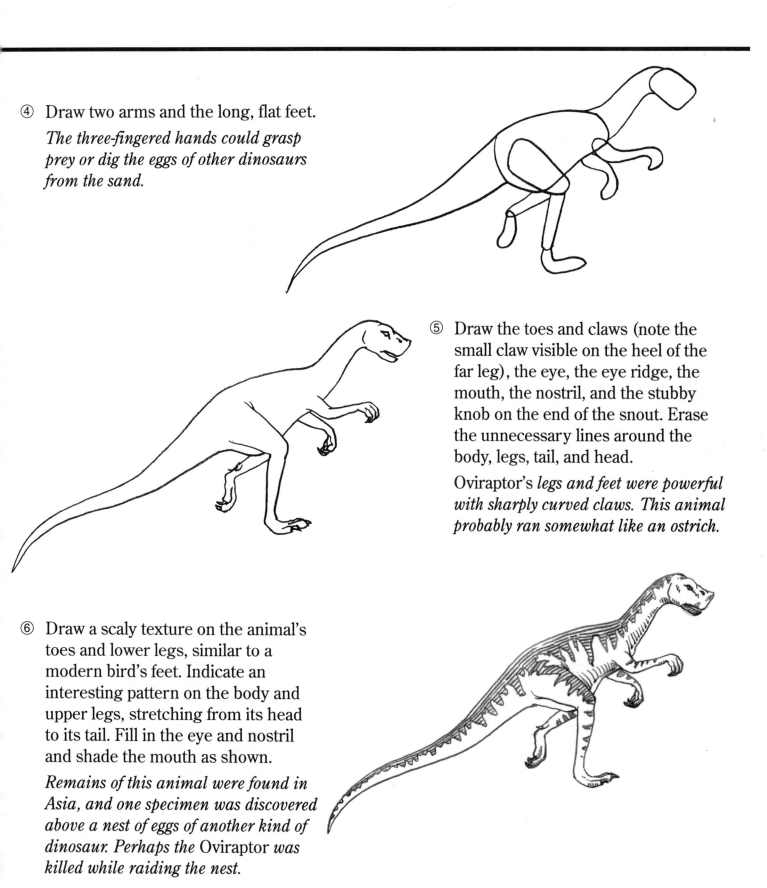

④ Draw two arms and the long, flat feet.

The three-fingered hands could grasp prey or dig the eggs of other dinosaurs from the sand.

⑤ Draw the toes and claws (note the small claw visible on the heel of the far leg), the eye, the eye ridge, the mouth, the nostril, and the stubby knob on the end of the snout. Erase the unnecessary lines around the body, legs, tail, and head.

Oviraptor's legs and feet were powerful with sharply curved claws. This animal probably ran somewhat like an ostrich.

⑥ Draw a scaly texture on the animal's toes and lower legs, similar to a modern bird's feet. Indicate an interesting pattern on the body and upper legs, stretching from its head to its tail. Fill in the eye and nostril and shade the mouth as shown.

Remains of this animal were found in Asia, and one specimen was discovered above a nest of eggs of another kind of dinosaur. Perhaps the Oviraptor *was killed while raiding the nest.*

DRAWING TIP: Paleontologists have compared *Oviraptor's* legs and feet to those of the ostrich. Notice how each animal has a claw on its heels. Are there any other similarities? What would your *Oviraptor* look like if it had feathers?

Deinonychus was a carnivorous dinosaur that lived in North

① To begin *Deinonychus*, draw the small body shape.

At 10 to 13 feet long, Deinonychus was not large compared to some of its relatives. Its skeleton reveals that it was probably a fierce predator.

② Sketch in an oval for the head. Attach the head to the body with a curved neckline. Extend the tail line horizontally from the body.

Almost three-fourths of Deinonychus's long tail was stiffened by bony rods that grew out of each tailbone.

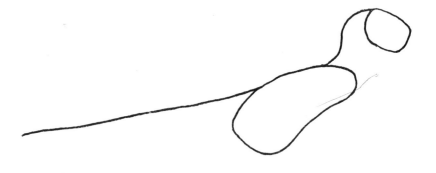

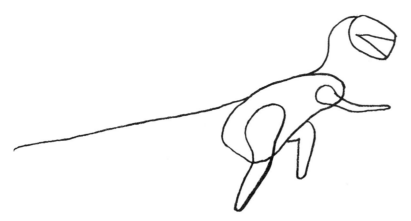

③ Then draw the legs, arm, and a V shape for the open jaw of this aggressive predator.

The long, muscular legs indicate that Deinonychus *was speedy and probably chased down its prey.*

MORE SCIENCE: *Deinonychus* used its long tail for balance as it ran at speeds of up to 30 miles per hour.

America toward the end of the age of dinosaurs. Its name means "terrible claw."

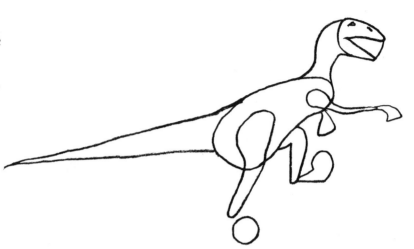

④ Now add the eye and nostril. Draw the lower neck and the underside of the tail. Add outlines for the clawed hands and feet.

For a dinosaur, Deinonychus *had a comparatively large brain. Although most of this capacity was devoted to the senses, it's likely that* Deinonychus *was relatively intelligent. It probably hunted in packs.*

⑤ Draw the ear hole. Add jagged rows of upper and lower teeth. Now draw in the claws as shown. Note the one huge claw on each foot. Erase all unnecessary lines around the head, body, limbs, and tail.

The five-inch claws on the second toe of each hindfoot could have allowed Deinonychus *to easily slash the belly of a much larger beast.*

⑥ Fill in the eye and add a tongue in the animal's mouth. Shade the body and limb contours to suggest smooth scales. Finally, add highlight features in the claws to make them look very sharp. You can make *Deinonychus* look very real by leaving white space around the top of its body and tail.

Deinonychus *probably ran and jumped with great agility. It may have been a warm-blooded creature similar in some ways to today's birds.*

Gallimimus was a carnivorous reptile that was the largest of the "ostrich-like" dinosaurs. It walked on two legs and may

① To start your *Gallimimus*, sketch its body.

Found in eastern Asia, Gallimimus *grew up to 20 feet in length.*

② Begin drawing the neck and tail by making one curved line starting above the body, crossing the top, and extending outward. Sketch in a small oval for the upper foreleg and a large one for the upper hindleg.

Gallimimus *had a long, strong tail, which it used to help it balance as it ran swiftly.*

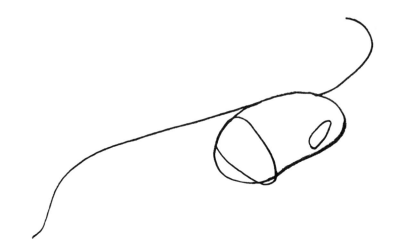

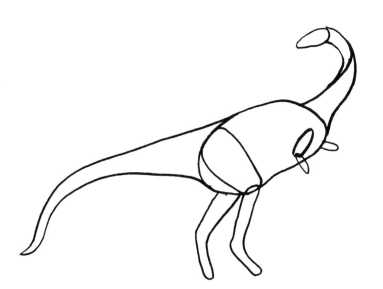

③ Next sketch in the tiny head. Draw in the necklines and the underside of the tail. The neck should look as if it is twisting around. Add the lower legs and forearms.

For a dinosaur, Gallimimus *had unusually large eyes and a large brain cavity.*

MORE SCIENCE: Some scientists believe *Gallimimus* was one of the fastest dinosaurs, easily reaching speeds of up to 35 miles per hour.

have dug up other dinosaurs' eggs to eat.

④ Draw in the feet and hands. You now have the complete outline for *Gallimimus*.

Gallimimus *was probably a speedy, efficient hunter. The long, slender legs were made for sprinting.*

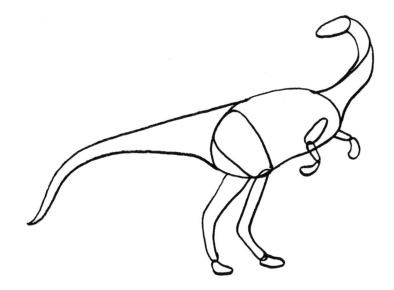

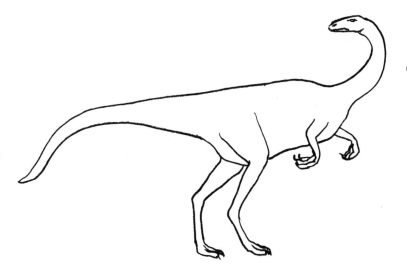

⑤ Now add the eye, nostril, and mouth. Detail the feet and hands with long toes and claws. Erase all the unneeded lines in the neck, body, legs, and tail.

Despite Gallimimus's *lack of teeth, it may have eaten small animals and insects.*

⑥ Use thick hatching to create depth and dimension. Shade in the undersides of the neck and body. You can create a smooth skin for *Gallimimus* by smearing your pencil marks with a tissue. Be sure to leave some white space for a three-dimensional look.

Gallimimus *means "rooster mimic." It got its name because of its resemblance to modern birds.*

Tyrannosaurus was the largest meat-eating animal we have ever known. When it stood fully erect, it was about 20

① First draw an irregular-shaped oval for the body of this mighty dinosaur.

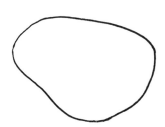

Tyrannosaurus *walked on two stout legs. Its thick, strong tail was held out straight to balance its body as it walked.*

② Sketch in a smaller oval for the head and connect it to the body with a short, curved neckline. Then add a longer curved line for the tail. Draw two small ovals for the tiny upper arms.

Tyrannosaurus *might have weighed anywhere between four to eight tons.*

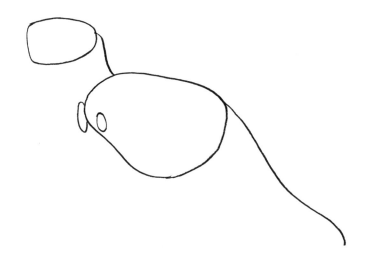

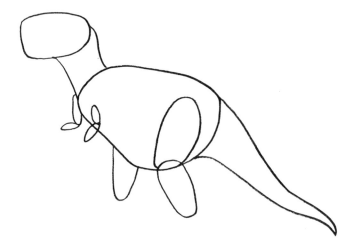

③ Add lines for the underside of the neck and tail. Draw in the upper hindleg, the two lower legs, and the two forearms.

The jaws of Tyrannosaurus *held flesh-tearing fangs that were saw-edged and up to six inches long.*

MORE SCIENCE: In dinosaur terms, both *Tyrannosaurus* species lived for only a "short" time—less than 10 million years.

feet tall and 39 feet long. It was probably an agile runner and a fierce hunter.

④ Now outline the huge feet and indicate the small, curved hands.

The puny forelimbs of this powerful dinosaur remain a puzzle to scientists. Even if Tyrannosaurus *used its fingers to catch prey, its arms were too short to reach its mouth. Scientists have suggested that* Tyrannosaurus *may have used these limbs to balance itself when standing up from a reclining position.*

⑤ Use a V shape to indicate the mouth and add two humps on top of its head to show where the eyes will be. Add the eye and nostril. Indicate the chest with a curved line above the forelimb. Add toes and claws to the hindfeet and thin claws at the end of each arm. Define the creature's underside with a line from the chest to the tail. Erase all unneeded lines.

Scientists believe that Tyrannosaurus *fed upon plant-eating hadrosaurs that lived in North America.*

⑥ Draw in horizontal lines along *Tyrannosaurus's* underside, then sketch in fine cross-hatching. To contour the body, limbs, and tail, use strokes that follow the dinosaur's curves. Last, fill in the eye and the nostril, and shade in the teeth and claws.

Scientists have identified at least two species of Tyrannosaurus: Tyrannosaurus luanchuanensis, *found in China, and* Tyrannosaurus rex, *found only in North America.*

DRAWING TIP: Although the iguana is a plant eater, its head and skin could be used as models for drawing *Tyrannosaurus,* "the tyrant lizard."

Spinosaurus had elongated bones in its spine, which supported a

① Begin by drawing a bean-shaped body for your *Spinosaurus.*

Spinosaurus *lived in what is now northern Africa and grew to about 39 feet in length.*

② Now sketch in the head. Connect it to the body with a curved neckline, and for the tail, extend a line downward past the body. Add the upper hindleg and the upper foreleg.

Among the largest of the known dinosaur carnivores, Spinosaurus *weighed up to seven tons—nearly the weight of the largest* Tyrannosaurus *(page 24).*

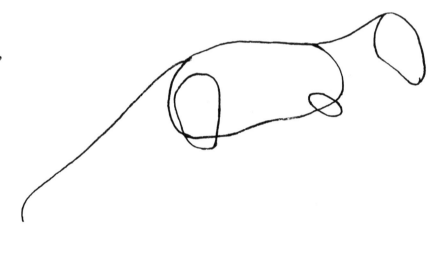

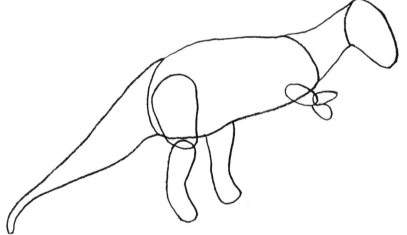

③ Complete the neck and tail with lines as shown. Add the four limbs.

Spinosaurus *walked upright on its muscular hindlegs. It used its smaller forelegs to aid in capturing prey.*

MORE SCIENCE: The name *Spinosaurus* means "spine reptile."

tall, upright sail on its back. *Spinosaurus* **lived during the Cretaceous period.**

④ Now sketch an outline for the top of the sail. Draw an eye and an open mouth. Add foot and hand shapes for this huge creature.

The sail on this creature's back was taller than a man and was probably used to regulate body heat. When turned toward the sun, the sail would absorb heat. When turned away, aided by cool breezes, it radiated heat.

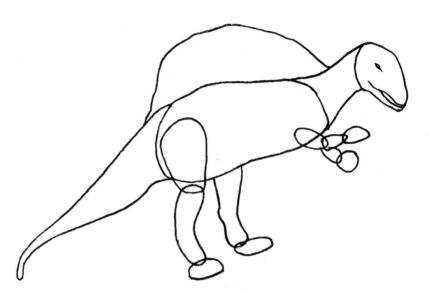

⑤ Indicate spine lines on the sail and add toes and sharp claws. Erase all unnecessary lines. Be careful not to erase any of the sail spines.

Some believe Spinosaurus's *sail was brightly colored and used to attract a mate.*

⑥ Indicate teeth and fill in the eye and nose. Create texture and dimension using hatching, which should be thicker for shaded areas. Last, shade in the claws.

Unusual for a meat eater, Spinosaurus's *teeth were not curved, but straight.*

Apatosaurus was one of the plant-eating dinosaurs that lived during the late Jurassic period (the Jurassic period

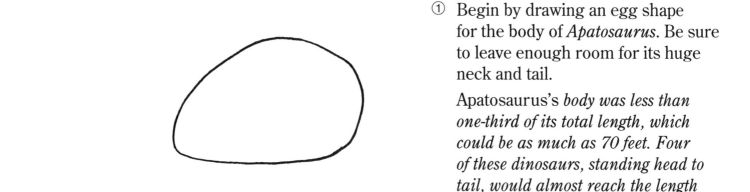

① Begin by drawing an egg shape for the body of *Apatosaurus*. Be sure to leave enough room for its huge neck and tail.

Apatosaurus's body was less than one-third of its total length, which could be as much as 70 feet. Four of these dinosaurs, standing head to tail, would almost reach the length of a football field.

② Next draw a long, curved line for the neck, which should be approximately the same length as the body. Add the tiny head and sketch in a curving line for the tail.

In spite of its great bulk, Apatosaurus may have, on rare occasions, raised itself on its back legs to fight off an attacker or to reach for food in the treetops.

③ Sketch in the four sturdy legs. Draw curved lines on the undersides of the neck and tail. The neck widens where it joins the body and the tail narrows as it reaches the end.

After the excavation of the bones of Apatosaurus *and other dinosaurs, Woodrow Wilson, then president of the United States, set aside 80 acres in Utah as an "American Antiquity," called Dinosaur National Monument. The year was 1915.*

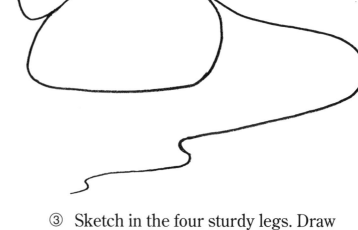

MORE SCIENCE: In order to sustain itself, this huge dinosaur probably ate more than 500 pounds of vegetation every day.

lasted from 208 million to 144 million years ago). The large group to which it belonged, called sauropoda, included the largest land animals that ever lived.

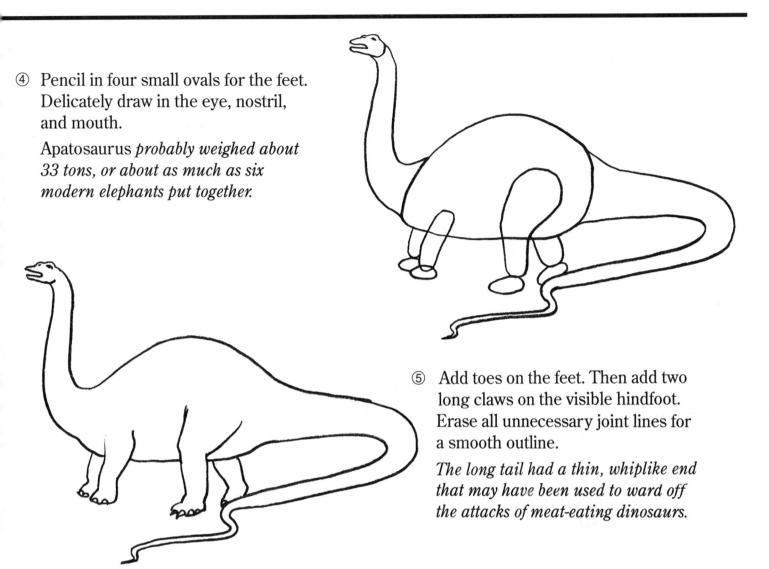

④ Pencil in four small ovals for the feet. Delicately draw in the eye, nostril, and mouth.

Apatosaurus *probably weighed about 33 tons, or about as much as six modern elephants put together.*

⑤ Add toes on the feet. Then add two long claws on the visible hindfoot. Erase all unnecessary joint lines for a smooth outline.

The long tail had a thin, whiplike end that may have been used to ward off the attacks of meat-eating dinosaurs.

⑥ Using short strokes, shade around the neck, body, tail, and legs to give it dimension. Notice that some strokes are little more than dots, while others are longer, particularly on the dinosaur's underside and far back leg. Last, add small, flat teeth inside its mouth.

Apatosaurus's *head, which was 22 inches in length, was tiny compared to its body. Its teeth were used chiefly to rake large quantities of leaves and twigs into its mouth.*

Pachycephalosaurus was a plant-eating dinosaur whose name means "thick-headed lizard."

① Begin by drawing the body of *Pachycephalosaurus* as shown.

Pachycephalosaurus remains have been found in Montana, South Dakota, and Wyoming. This dinosaur was 15 or more feet long, a giant among the boneheads.

② Now draw a circle for the head. Connect the head to the body with a curved line. Extend the tail straight out past the body.

The dome on top of Pachycephalosaurus's *head is due to its extremely thick skull. It is trimmed with knobs and spikes. Paleontologists believe that , similar to a modern ram, males butted heads with other males in the herd to establish territory and compete for mates.*

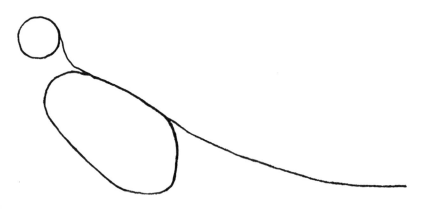

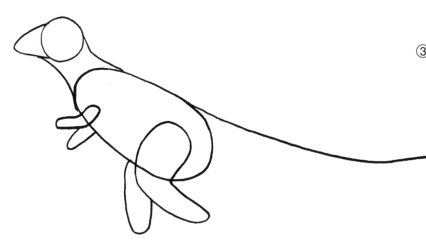

③ Add the snout and underside of the neck. Then draw the four limbs, with two of them slightly bent.

Pachycephalosaurus walked on two legs. It had five fingers on its hands and three toes on its feet.

MORE SCIENCE: *Pachycephalosaurus's* unusual skull measured as much as two feet in length.

Another name given to this prehistoric reptile is "bonehead"!

④ Now sketch the hands and feet. Add the underside of the tail.

Pachycephalosaurus *probably used its forelimbs to bring branches close enough for cropping.*

⑤ Detail the eye, nostril, and knobby spikes on the head and face. Draw the long digits and claws. Erase any unnecessary joint lines.

The bony cap on this animal's skull was 10 inches thick. Its backbone was specially structured to absorb the shock from head butting.

⑥ Use crosshatch lines to create contouring shadows and to suggest a lizardlike skin texture.

Pachycephalosaurus *lived until the very end of the age of dinosaurs.*

Pterodactylus was a prehistoric creature (not a dinosaur) that flew on "wings" made of skin. *Pterodactylus* lived

① To begin your *Pterodactylus*, draw a thin, leaf shape for the body.

Pterodactylus, *one of the best-known prehistoric flying reptiles, had a wingspan of about two feet, five inches. Its fossils have been found in Africa and Europe.*

② Add the head and two long, thin, slanting arms. Connect the head to the body with a short, upward-curving neck.

This creature's wing membrane was supported along the front edge by a very long fourth finger. The wing joined the body near the knee.

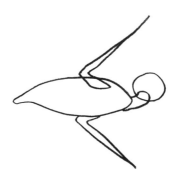

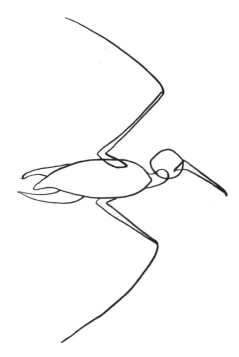

③ Next draw the upper triangular jaw and backward-curving lines for the rest of the front-wing edge. Add two hooked shapes for the hindlegs.

Most Pterodactylus *remains have been found in marine deposits, and scientists conclude that the prehistoric animal fed mainly on fish.*

MORE SCIENCE: *Pterodactylus* belonged to a group of flying reptiles that included the largest flying creature known. Called *Quetzalcoatlus*, this animal had a wingspan of up to 40 feet.

during the late Jurassic period, when some of the largest dinosaurs roamed the Earth.

---

④ Now draw the lower jaw. Sketch in outlines for the hands and feet. Complete the outline for the wings and add a thin line along the upper jaw as a guideline for the teeth.

Pterodactylus *had long, narrow jaws lined with sharp teeth for grasping prey.*

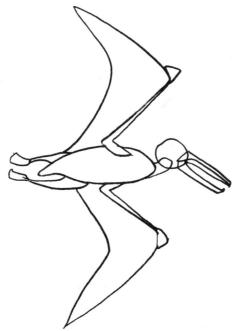

⑤ Put five small strokes on each foot for the toe claws. Draw three claws on each hand and add a small eye. Begin to sketch in fur lines around the shoulders and body. Erase all unneeded lines. Then add lines above the forelimbs, connecting them to the shoulders. Also add a thin line down each outside edge of the wings, ending the lines with a hook.

Some scientists think that this flying reptile was covered with fur.

⑥ Use small strokes to create scales on the head and legs, pointed teeth, and feathers around the neck area. Attach feathers to the long tailbone and to the wings. Note that the wing feathers are shorter near the front edge. Fill in the eye and add a nostril at the end of the jaw. Finally, sketch in very small V shapes on its body as shown.

Most paleontologists believe that Archaeopteryx *did fly or glide among trees, despite its small breastbone and lack of strong flight muscles. However, it is also believed to have been a strong runner, similar to a modern roadrunner.*

Pteranodon was one of the largest of the flying reptiles. It wasn't a dinosaur, but a pterosaur. It had a wingspan of some 23

① Begin by drawing a small leaf shape for *Pteranodon's* body.

Even though Pteranodon's *wings were enormous, scientists estimate that the creature weighed only about 37 pounds.*

② Then draw the head shape with its bony crest extending behind it. Now draw a curved line for the front edge of the huge wings.

The function of Pteranodon's *bony crest, which was sometimes as long as the head itself, is unknown. Perhaps it balanced out the animal's long, heavy skull or was used as a rudder during flight.*

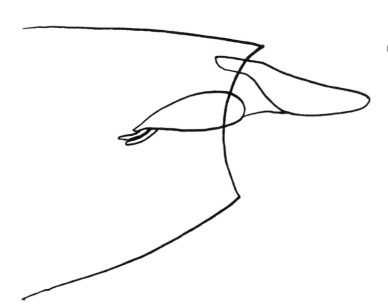

③ Add the thin legs, a line for the lower neck, and two lines stretching outward to indicate the side edges of the wings.

As with Pterodactylus *(page 32),* Pteranodon's *leathery wings were supported by a very long fourth claw on each hand.*

MORE SCIENCE: *Pteranodon* remains have been found in both Europe and North America.

feet and a bony crest atop its head that extended three feet, making the head six feet from end to end.

---

④ Draw the feet and hand shapes. Sketch a narrow V shape for the open beak and add another thin line to indicate the lower jaw. Sketch two curved lines to complete the outline of the wings. Notice how the far wing overlaps the crest, giving your flying reptile a three-dimensional look. Don't forget to add the upper side of the neck.

Pteranodon's great wings, which were much larger than its body, probably enabled the reptile to soar for long periods through the air instead of actively flying.

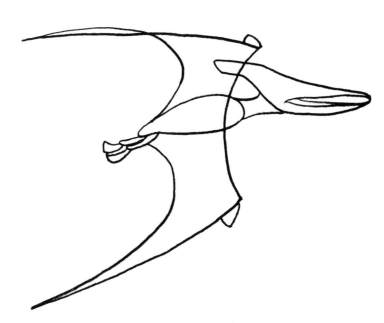

⑤ Pencil in the claws, the eye, and the nostril, which is in front of the eye. Add the thin arms, which are connected to its wings. Erase any unnecessary lines.

Unlike most of its relatives, Pteranodon was toothless. It probably fished the way a pelican does, swooping over water, scooping up its prey in its mouth, and swallowing it whole.

⑥ Fill in the eye, nostril, and mouth. Use a smattering of stippling for skin texture, concentrating it around the outline of the creature. Now watch it soar above the heads of other prehistoric animals!

Most remains of the flying reptiles give us little information about the texture of skin or whether it was covered by feathers or fur.

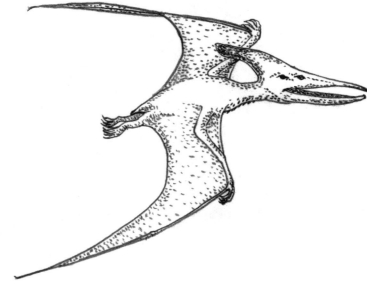

Archaeopteryx was the earliest known bird—that is, the earliest known animal proved to have had feathers. It

① Begin by drawing an egg-shaped body for this prehistoric animal.

Found in Europe, Archaeopteryx *was thought to have been 14 inches long, including its tail. The prehistoric bird probably fed on insects.*

② Next sketch in a long loop for the tail. Add a small head and connect it to the body with a short, curved neckline.

Distinct from birds of today, Archaeopteryx *had a long, bony tail with feathers attached.*

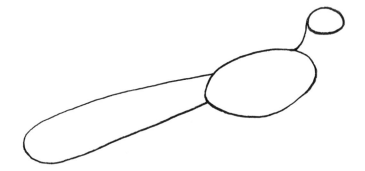

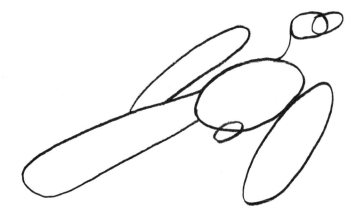

③ Draw two large ovals for the outer sections of the wings and add a small oval for one of the upper legs. Then add a small, rounded rectangle for its jaws.

Unlike modern birds, Archaeopteryx *did not have a beak, but long, slender jaws lined with sharp teeth.*

MORE SCIENCE: As with many birds, *Archaeopteryx* may have been colored to blend in with its forest surroundings. Some artists portray it as brightly colored as a parrot.

lived about 150 million years ago.

④ Indicate the eye and pencil in a V shape for the jaws. Connect the wing ovals to the body. Don't forget to add the other upper leg section to this two-legged animal. Add thin lower legs and two foot shapes.

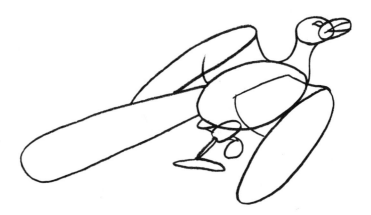

Archaeopteryx fossils were first found in a limestone quarry. They were so perfectly preserved that the impressions of its feathers were easy to see in the rock.

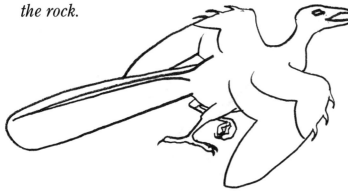

⑥ Use small, delicate strokes to create scales on the head and legs, small pointed teeth, and feathers around the neck area. Attach feathers to the long tailbone and to the wings. Note that the wing feathers are shorter near the front edge. Fill in the eye and add a nostril at the end of the jaw. Finally, sketch in very small V shapes on *Archaeopteryx's* body, making sure the tips point toward the tail.

Most paleontologists believe that Archaeopteryx *did fly or glide among trees, despite its small breastbone and lack of strong flight muscles. However, it is also believed to have been a strong runner, similar to a modern roadrunner.*

⑤ Now add toes and claws to the feet. Sketch in three tiny, clawed fingers on the front edge of *Archaeopteryx's* wings. Include a spine line down the center of the bony tail. Erase the unneeded lines. Add two wide V shapes on the wings, which will separate the shorter feathers from the longer ones.

The tiny clawed fingers on this creature's wings are similar to those on pterosaurs and on modern bats. Archaeopteryx *was most likely not a very strong flier and may have used its clawed fingers to climb trees.*

DRAWING TIP: You could think of this animal as a cross between a crow and a lizard—with both scales *and* feathers on its body.

Dimorphodon was an early pterosaur. *Dimorphodon* had leathery wings, and its long tail was tipped with a spade-

① Begin by drawing two separate egg shapes. The smaller one is the animal's head.

Dimorphodon *had a wingspan of about four feet.*

② To indicate the edges of the wings, draw a wide V shape. Connect the smaller head shape to the body with a curved, short neckline. Draw two fang-shaped legs.

Remains of Dimorphodon *were found in marine deposits in England. The wings were membranes of skin that were supported by an elongated fourth finger and anchored to the sides of the body.*

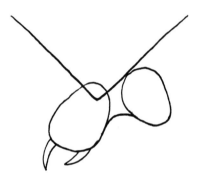

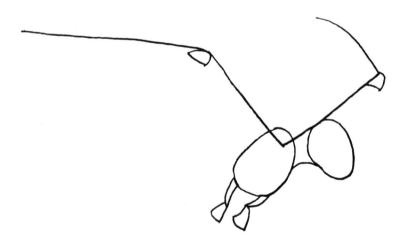

③ Next add two lines in a backward direction from each high point of the V shape. Draw triangular shapes for the hands and feet.

Dimorphodon *was an active flier and its leg structure, unusual for a pterosaur, indicates that it was able to walk quite capably, much like a modern bird.*

MORE SCIENCE: Scientists can find no reason for the large head and deep bill of this creature. Perhaps the bill was brightly colored and used as a courtship display similar to today's puffin and toucan birds.

shaped structure typical of flying reptiles of 190 million years ago.

④ In between its legs, add the tapering tail line and its triangular tail fin. Complete the neck and the wings as shown.

The small fin of skin at the end of its tail probably helped Dimorphodon *to steer in flight.*

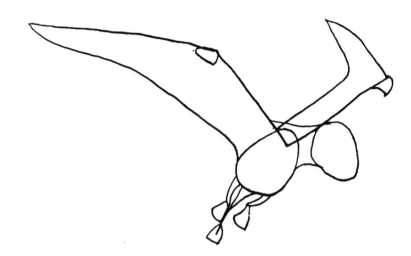

⑤ Indicate three fingers on each hand and five toes on each foot. Add the eye, the outline of the beak, the nostril, and one protruding tooth. (Its other large, spiky tooth is on the other side.) Erase all unnecessary and over-lapping joint lines.

Dimorphodon *means "two-form tooth" refering to its long, spiky front teeth and its abundant, small rear teeth.*

⑥ Last, add long arms running along each wing. If desired, shade the wings with parallel lines. Use light, feathery strokes around its body to indicate fur. A bright pattern on the beak would complete *Dimorphodon* nicely—don't forget to shade the tail and eye.

There is still uncertainty about whether pterosaurs were warm-blooded. If so, it is possible their bodies were covered by a fine coat of fur as shown here.

Lambeosaurus belonged to a large family of plant-eating dinosaurs called hadrosaurs. The hadrosaurs

① Begin your *Lambeosaurus* by drawing a bean shape for the body.

Lambeosaurus, *on average, grew to be 30 feet long, including its tail. The fossils of one giant specimen found in California indicate that it may have been 54 feet long—the largest duckbill dinosaur ever discovered.*

② Draw a small pear-shaped head and connect it to the body with a short, curved stroke. Then extend this line outward past the body to suggest a tail. Indicate the upper legs and the upper arm.

Lambeosaurus, *which weighed three tons, used its tail for balance as it ran through its forest home.*

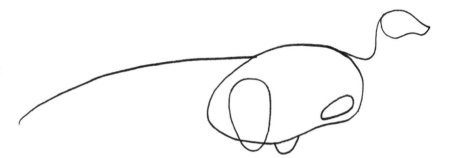

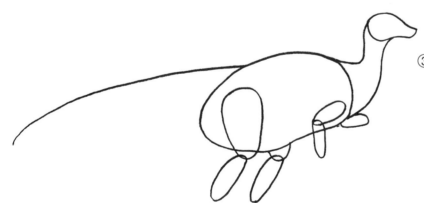

③ Draw a line to indicate the underside of the neck. Sketch in the lower parts of the leg, the far upper arm, and the near forearm.

Lambeosaurus *had long, strong hindlimbs and shorter forelimbs. Each toe had a hooflike claw.*

MORE SCIENCE: Although both the male and female *Lambeosaurus* probably had crests, those of the males may have been larger and more elaborate.

were known for their flattened snouts, which looked something like a duck's bill.

---

④ Next add the feet and hands. Detail the bill with a short line. Sketch in a curved, pointed horn and a wider, curved crest in front of it.

Lambeosaurus's mouth ended in a toothless beak. On either side of its mouth, however, it had several rows of teeth arranged like a food grater.

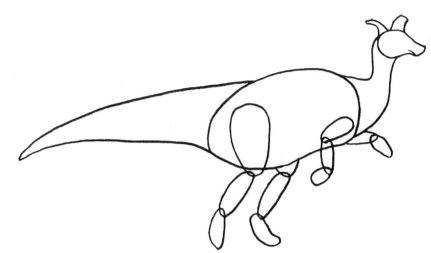

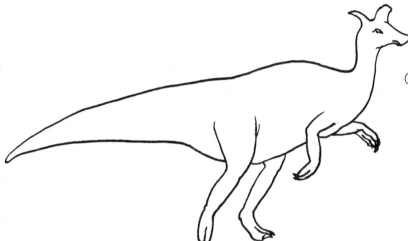

⑤ Indicate the long toes and claws and add an eye. Erase any unnecessary joint lines around the head, body, tail, and legs.

When alarmed, Lambeosaurus probably stood up on its hindlegs to get a better look before sprinting away.

⑥ You are now ready to add texture to your *Lambeosaurus*. Add a horizontal row of hatch lines in the tail to indicate musculature. To give this creature a smooth, scaly look, draw in dark, short strokes—closer together in the shaded areas and farther apart along the back, face, and arms. Finally, fill in the eye.

Lambeosaurus had a two-part crest. Its backward-pointing spike was solid. The rectangular bony crest on its forehead was hollow. Scientists believe this hollow crest was used to produce loud calls.

Parasaurolophus was among the strangest of the duckbill dinosaurs. Within its up to six-foot-long

① First draw *Parasaurolophus's* body shape.

Parasaurolophus grew to about 33 feet in length.

② Draw a small head and connect it to the body with a short curved line. Extend the tail outward past the body. Draw the two visible upper legs. Notice how the reptile's head is slightly lower than its back.

Like the other duckbill dinosaurs, Parasaurolophus's hindlegs were much longer than its front legs. It used its long, strong tail for balance.

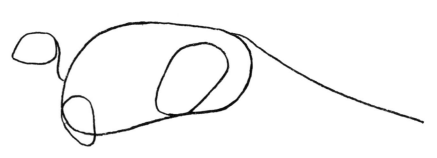

③ Now draw lines for the undersides of the tail and the neck. Add the four lower legs.

The very thick tail may have been brightly colored. If so, it could have been used as a device to signal danger, to attract mates, or to help members of a herd recognize each other.

MORE SCIENCE: The feet of *Parasaurolophus* were similar to the fast-running feet and toes of the modern ostrich. The feet were probably covered with thick scaly skin.

crest, two slender, tubelike nasal passages swept back from the nostrils for the full extent of the crest, then curved back toward the snout.

④ Next add the eye, nostrils, and the lower corner of the short bill. Then draw the curved crest above the head. Insert a small notch in the animal's back and add the feet.

The interesting internal structure of Parasaurolophus's *crest may have permitted the dinosaur to snort as loudly as a foghorn to call to its herd.*

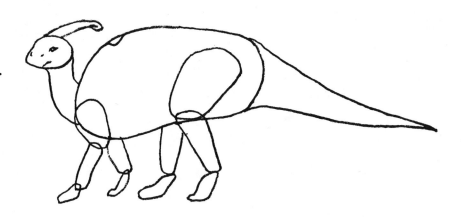

⑤ Fill in the eye and suggest the other eye with a small ridge. Add details to the toes and claws. Erase all unnecessary lines and smooth the joint lines. Begin to suggest dimension with creases between *Parasaurolophus's* upper legs and its body.

The notch in Parasaurolophus's *spine is an unusual feature. Based on its location, some scientists have guessed that the notch provided a slot for the crest. If so, when the animal arched its neck backward as it hurried through the brush, the crest would sweep the thick branches up and out of the way.*

⑥ Complete the duckbill by drawing two lines around the nostrils and back toward the long crest. Shade your creature by using short hatching along its back and legs and longer, darker hatching on its tail, neck, and undersides. Last, shade the claws.

Parasaurolophus, *like the other duckbills, lived on a diet of seeds, leaves, and stems.*

Stegosaurus was a plant-eating dinosaur that lived 140 million years ago. Its memorable feature was the double row

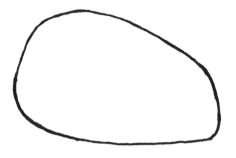

① First draw an egg for the body as shown.

Stegosaurus's *body was a full 30 feet long from nose to tail.*

② Next add the tail, neck, and head shapes.

Although Stegosaurus's *head was about the size of a horse's head, its brain was no bigger than a walnut!*

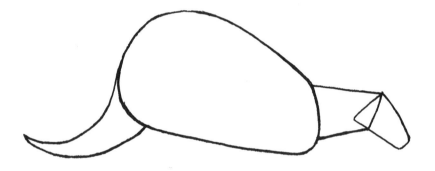

③ Now add the leg shapes. Notice the very stout, long hindlegs and the shorter front legs. Add shapes for the two feet nearest you.

Stegosaurus's *front legs were shorter than its hindlegs. This arrangement leads scientists to believe that this dinosaur was a slow-moving creature.*

MORE SCIENCE: *Stegosaurus's* largest plates were three feet high and three feet wide.

of bony plates that covered its neck, back, and tail.

④ Next draw a light line above the back as a guide, then add a row of diamond-shaped plates. The guideline is to help you taper the row of plates properly.

Stegosaurus probably used its sharp, bony plates to help regulate its body temperature by turning them toward or away from the sun.

⑤ Erase the joint lines within the body so it is a smooth, clean shape. Then add the eye, mouth, toes, and toenails, a second row of plates on the back, and four spikes on the tail.

The tail spikes were straight, sharp, and about three feet long. On the tip of a strong, flexible tail, the spikes made a very powerful weapon against attackers.

⑥ Add hatching on the body, tail, neck, and head. Shade the plates with straight lines as shown, and draw hatch marks on the body to show where the plates cast shadows.

Scientists think Stegosaurus *had tough, scaly skin. It may have been brightly colored, or it may have been green or brown to help camouflage the animal among the trees.*

DRAWING TIP: Before you draw *Stegosaurus's* skin, try to find a picture of a scaly lizard to look at. *Stegosaurus's* skin was probably very similar to the modern reptile's skin.

Ankylosaurus was a plant-eating dinosaur covered with armored plates. More fully armored than *Stegosaurus,*

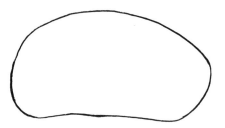

① First draw a rounded rectangle for the body of *Ankylosaurus.*

Ankylosaurus *was built like a tank and may have grown up to 25 feet in length.*

② Now draw a triangular head using curved lines as shown. Extend a curved tail line past the body. Draw a circle at the end of the tail to form a club shape.

Ankylosaurus *undoubtedly used its bony knob tail club to swing at enemies to keep them away or disable those that came too close.*

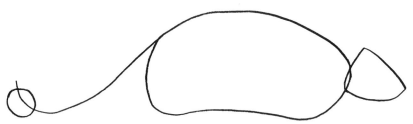

③ Next indicate the tail's rounded tip and underside. Draw in the four sturdy legs.

Ankylosaurus *was powerfully built to support its weight of up to four tons.*

MORE SCIENCE: *Ankylosaurus* lived in what is now western North America.

(page 44), *Ankylosaurus* **also had a huge bony knob on its tail.**

④ Add the upper and lower necklines. Next draw the eye, the nostril, the mouth, and the triangular spikes around the head. Sketch in the feet.

Ankylosaurus's *mouth ended in a toothless beak.*

⑤ Pencil in the toes and claws. Erase all unnecessary lines on your creature and detail the tail club as shown. Draw curved lines from the head to the tail to indicate the separate rows of armor plates.

This dinosaur may have used its sharp claws to dig for roots to eat.

⑥ Now it's time to add the armor. Cross the lines you've already drawn with shorter lines running from the top of the body to the underside. Draw a backward-curving spike inside each square as shown. Note that the spikes are smaller toward the tail. Cross-hatch around the legs, face, and tail. Shade the spikes and the tail club, and fill in the eye and nostril. Give the tail texture by adding tiny triangles in the lower portion as shown.

Ankylosaurus's *armor consisted of plates made of a bony material formed into bumps and spikes that covered its back, sides, neck, and tail.*

DRAWING TIP: If possible, study the skin of a crocodile before drawing the outside of *Ankylosaurus.* Imitate the crocodile's squarish plates and centered bumps on its back and tail.

Chasmosaurus was a ceratopsian, or horned dinosaur. It was the

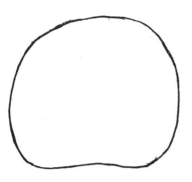

① Begin by drawing a rounded square for the body of your *Chasmosaurus*.

Remains of Chasmosaurus *have been found in southern Canada. These dinosaurs may have grown up to 17 feet in length.*

② Now draw the U-shaped outline for the frill. Add the thick tail.

The spectacular frill of Chasmosaurus *was longer than the skull itself. The frill, a fan-shaped bony plate on the back of its skull, was probably used for display, either to scare off enemies or to impress other herd members.*

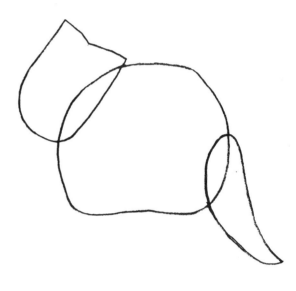

③ Next draw the large blunt snout and the thick legs.

Chasmosaurus's *stocky legs were designed to bear a great deal of weight.*

MORE SCIENCE: Some of the *Chasmosaurus* specimens that have been found do not have the long brow horns that this one does, although their remains were similar in most other ways. It is possible that these short-horned creatures were females.

earliest known dinosaur to develop a very long, bony neck frill.

④ Add the three horns on its forehead. Draw circular shapes for the feet. Sketch curved lines from the bases of the horns to the top of the frill.

Some paleontologists believe that Chasmosaurus *could move quite quickly despite its great weight. That's because its shoulder blades weren't firmly attached by bone (or by bony connections) to its skeleton and weren't restrained by a collarbone.*

⑤ Pencil in the eye and eye ridge and the nostril and nostril ridge. Draw in the toes and the hooflike claws. Complete the frill by creating a notch in it near the neck. Add the mouth and the beak at the end of its snout. Connect the lower part of the head with the body. Erase all unneeded lines.

It's frill, unlike Triceratops's, *was not solid bone but a framework supported by muscle and skin. This indicates that it was probably not used for protection.*

⑥ Add pointed knobs along the frill's edge and then darken them. The skin was probably thick and leathery like an elephant's, so use cross-hatching to shade around the creature's face, legs, underside, and tail. Fill in the eye and nostril and add details to the dangerous horns and claws.

Its name means "ravine" or "opening reptile" which refers to the openings in Chasmosaurus's *frill.*

DRAWING TIP: Chasmosaurus's *frill may have been used to attract a mate or frighten away predators. In either case, the frill may have been brightly colored like the throat pouches of some modern birds and frogs. Give your* Chasmosaurus *some color and decorate its frill!*

Styracosaurus was a smaller relative of *Triceratops* (page 52) and a slightly larger relative of *Chasmosaurus*

① First draw a rounded shape for the body of *Styracosaurus*.

Styracosaurus's *fossils have been found in Montana and southern Canada. Styracosaurus grew from 17 to 18 feet in length, and it weighed about four tons.*

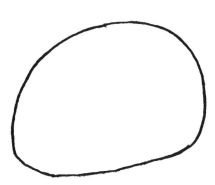

② Now draw the peanut-shaped head and the triangular tail.

Styracosaurus's *legs were short and thick, which may indicate that it walked with a slow but powerful gait. Its stocky toes were capped with hooflike claws.*

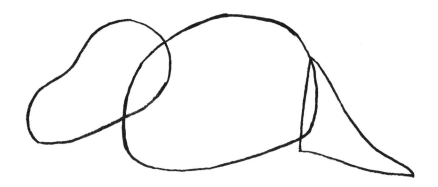

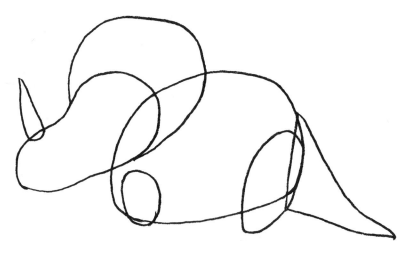

③ Sketch an outline for the animal's crown of horns. Then add the nose horn and upper legs.

Although this dinosaur's skull and frill were large, the openings in the frill kept the head light enough to move easily.

MORE SCIENCE: *Styracosaurus's* frill had six main spikes, the longest of which was more than two feet in length.

(page 48). Of the group to which all three of these dinosaurs belonged, the ceratopsians, *Styracosaurus* had one of the most spectacular frills.

④ Pencil in the eye, the nostril, and the lower edge of the beak. Add a thin line for the lower jaw and connect the head and chest with a line for the neck. Add the four lower legs.

Styracosaurus's two-and-a-half-foot-long nose horn, which pointed straight up, made this dinosaur quite spectacular. The horn may have been used to rip open the belly of an attacking meat eater.

⑤ Next draw the spikes and horns in varying lengths around the frill as shown. Indicate the ridge of the far eye. Detail the toes and hooflike claws and erase any unnecessary lines.

The long spikes on Styracosaurus's *frill were a good protection from predators and probably were used in defensive displays or to attract mates.*

⑥ Use the side of a pencil to shade in contours on the underside of the body and legs. Shade in the area around the frill ridge as well. Note that several of the spikes cast shadows.

Styracosaurus in Greek means "spiked reptile."

Triceratops

means "three-horned face." It was one of a large group of horned dinosaurs called ceratopsians. The ceratopsians lived during the Cretaceous period, which

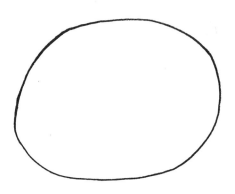

① To begin, draw a wide oval for the body.

Triceratops's body structure is similar to that of today's rhinoceros. But it was up to 30 feet long and weighed anywhere from six to eight tons. The modern rhino is about 12 feet long and weighs about four tons.

② Now draw a circular shape for the back part of its head. Sketch in a thick, curved tail.

A special characteristic of Triceratops was the frill on the back of its skull. The frill was thinly covered with skin and helped protect the animal's neck when it was attacked.

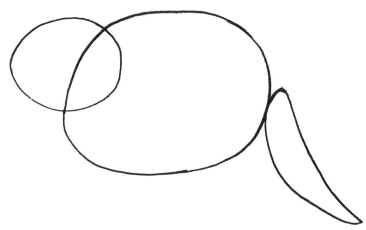

③ Next draw the round beak, overlapping it with the head. Add three horns: two above *Triceratops's* eyes, one on its snout. Sketch the thick legs, which are shorter in the front.

Triceratops had a thick, short nose horn. The horns over its eyes, however, were as long as three feet.

MORE SCIENCE: *Triceratops* traveled in large herds, probably with the young safely at the center of the group. That way, the young were protected from dangerous meat eaters.

lasted from 144 million to 65 million years ago. *Triceratops* **lived at the very end of the period, between 70 million and 65 million years ago.**

④ Suggest the edges of the beak and the mouth with small, curved lines. Indicate the lower edge of the neck and add four wedge shapes for the feet.

Triceratops *used its beak to clip a meal of leaves and twigs. It had shearing teeth at the back of its jaws for cutting the tough plant material.*

⑤ Now pencil in the face details: the small eye, the ridge joining the front and back horns, and the nostril. Indicate a notch in the frill near the cheek. Add claws. Erase any unnecessary lines for a smooth body contour. Begin to indicate dimension by adding small creases at the joints between the legs and the body.

Triceratops's *claws were not sharply pointed. Instead, they were rather blunt and hooflike.*

⑥ Use dark, curved hatching around the frill, under the head, on the two far legs, and underneath the belly and tail. Use lighter hatching around the back and face and along the two nearest legs. Fill in the eye and shade the claws and horns. Add spiked knobs around the frill's edge, then shade them as shown.

Some scientists suggest that Triceratops's *frill anchored tremendous jaw muscles that gave the dinosaur a bite powerful enough to snap a two-inch-thick branch.*

DRAWING TIP: Paleontologists think that *Triceratops's* joints and leg bones were similar to those of modern elephants and rhinos. Study the shape and thickness of these animals' legs to help you draw *Triceratops*.

Shonisaurus was not a dinosaur, but the largest known of the ichthyosaurs, or "fish lizards." It lived at the

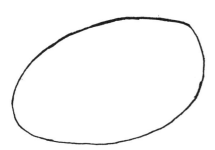

① Begin your *Shonisaurus* by drawing a large oval for the body.

Shonisaurus *was about 49 feet long, longer than a four-story building is tall!*

② Next draw a pointed, triangular head and jaws. Sketch in a rectangular tail, which widens as it connects to the body.

The long, beaklike jaws of this fish eater were equipped with front teeth only.

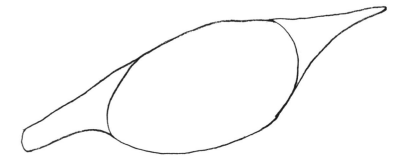

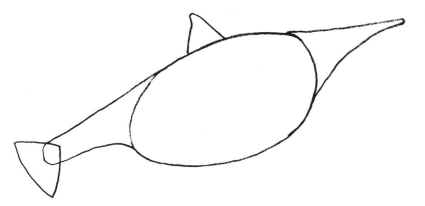

③ Now draw a triangle on this reptile's back for a dorsal fin, which helped it to balance. Add a fan-shaped triangle on the end for the tail.

Unlike many other sea reptiles, including Kronosaurus *(see page 56),* Shonisaurus *did not come ashore to lay eggs. Instead, it gave birth to live young in the sea, the way dolphins and whales do today.*

MORE SCIENCE: Although *Shonisaurus* was a marine reptile, its fossil remains were found in the state of Nevada! That's because when *Shonisaurus* lived, around 220 million years ago, Nevada lay under a great inland sea.

beginning of the age of dinosaurs. *Shonisaurus* **looked like and ate fish, but was in fact a seagoing, air-breathing reptile.**

④ Sketch the four lower fins that probably helped it to steer.

Shonisaurus *used its flippers to help it move forward, but, as with modern fish, its tail provided the power for most of the forward motion.*

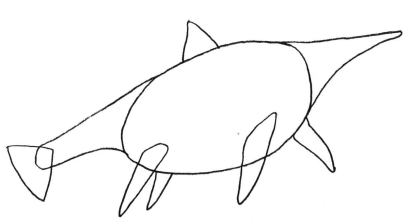

⑤ Pencil in the eye, the nostril, and the long mouth line (*Shonisaurus* looks almost like it is smiling). Erase all unnecessary lines around the fins, tail, and head.

Unlike fish whose fins are thin and flexible, the flippers of Shonisaurus *were rigid and all the same size.*

⑥ To indicate smooth skin texture, use the side of the pencil to rub a smooth shadow below each feature or curved line. To get an even smoother look, you may want to rub your pencil marks with a tissue. Notice how *Shonisaurus* is darker around its underside, far fins, and tail fin. Don't forget to fill in the eye and nostril.

This sea reptile did not have scales, but a smooth skin, similar to today's dolphins.

Kronosaurus

was the heaviest of the plesiosaurs, which were not dinosaurs, but prehistoric reptiles that lived in the

① To begin your *Kronosaurus*, draw a long, flat oval for the body.

Kronosaurus *had a thick body supported by heavy ribs. Scientists think that one reason this marine lizard had such heavy ribs may have been to support its great weight if it crawled out of the water to lay eggs onshore.*

② Now draw a rectangular shape for the head. Sketch a line from the back of the head to the body, extending it past the body to form a slightly upcurved tail.

Kronosaurus's *head was nearly nine feet long, or almost one-quarter of its 42-foot length. Its head was larger and stronger than that of the largest land-living meat eaters.*

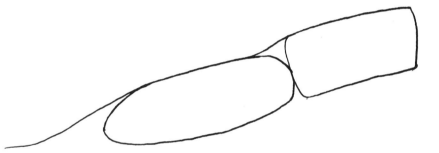

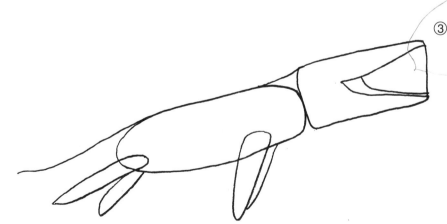

③ Add the front and back flippers. Draw a V shape for the open mouth. Draw an extra line inside the mouth to indicate the far side of the lower jaw.

Kronosaurus's *flipperlike limbs were similar in shape to the wings of today's penguins.* Kronosaurus *probably flapped its flippers to "fly" through the water.*

MORE SCIENCE: What's the easiest way to tell that *Kronosaurus* was not a dinosaur? It lived in the water, and there were no seagoing dinosaurs.

ocean and whose limbs were modified into fins. *Kronosaurus* **hunted huge sharks and squid.**

---

④ Add lines for the bottom of the tail, the lower edge of the neck, and the curved top of the snout.

Kronosaurus *swam where the continent of Australia now sits. At that time—around 130 million years ago— parts of Australia were flooded by warm shallow seas, where* Kronosaurus *lived and hunted.*

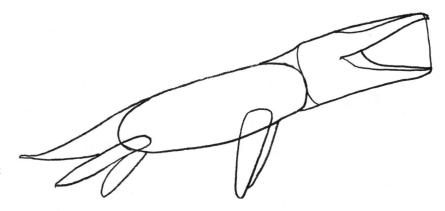

⑤ Pencil in the eye, the nostril in front of it, and the sharp teeth. Erase all unnecessary lines around the head, body, tail, and flippers.

In spite of its tremendous size and bulk, Kronosaurus *was probably swift and agile in the water.*

⑥ Now it's time to shade in this ancient reptile. Use the side of your pencil to create a soft, shadowy look and light, short hatch lines to define the body. Fill in the eye and the gaping mouth and add a small ear hole behind the jaw. Finally, shade in the teeth to make them look sharp and ferocious!

The skin of Kronosaurus *was probably smooth, similar to that of a modern killer whale or dolphin.*

Bringing Your Prehistoric Animal to Life

Here are more tips to putting life into your drawings. Keep in mind that the most realistic drawings combine several finishing techniques. You can practice and experiment with your own favorite combinations!

CONTOUR DRAWING

Even if you don't plan to fill in your drawing with color or texture, you can make your dinosaurs and other prehistoric creatures look more solid by changing the darkness and width of their outlines. For example, note the difference in line weight within the drawing of *Tyrannosaurus*. The lower edges around the animal are thicker and the upper outline is thinner, making *Tyrannosaurus* look as if it will stomp off the page!

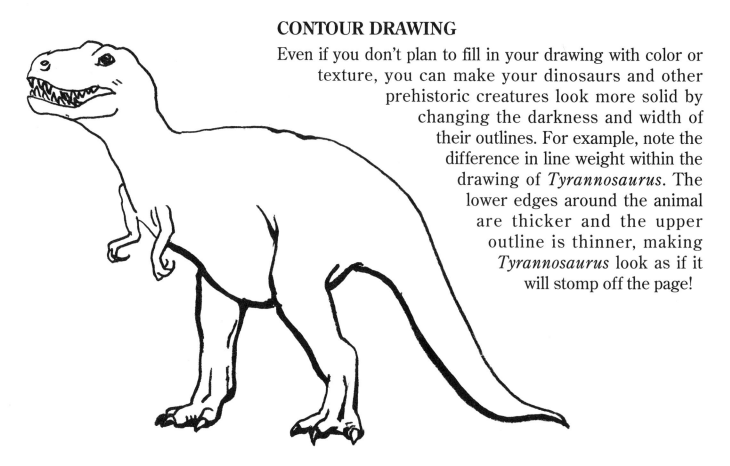

CAST SHADOWS

Your drawings will look much more realistic if some ground is added for the animals to stand on. Begin drawing a horizontal line at ground level. Then thicken the line to make it look like a full shadow, as shown with *Tyrannosaurus*. Make the shadow thinner under narrow body parts and thicker under fuller body parts. Shadows can also appear on the underside of the animal itself, not just on the ground. The heavy line on the underside of *Tyrannosaurus* enhances the shadow effect.

LIGHT FIGURE, DARK BACKGROUND

You'll be surprised by how rounded your prehistoric creature looks if you simply darken the space behind it. You can imagine the animal standing at the edge of a dark forest. Of course, if you add some shadows underneath the animal, the effect is even stronger—as with *Tyrannosaurus*!

Making Your Dinosaur Seem Larger (or Smaller)

How do you make a dinosaur in a small drawing seem larger? Or a dinosaur in a huge picture seem smaller?

THE HORIZON LINE

To show how big your creature is in a drawing, add a ground or horizon line across your picture. The horizon line is on the viewer's eye level. So, if the horizon is near the bottom of your page and the dinosaur stretches far above it, as with *Apatosaurus*, the viewer will imagine it as large. If you draw in a horizon line near the top section of your picture, *Apatosaurus* will appear much smaller.

ADDING OBJECTS

Another way is to include objects whose size most people know. Fully grown trees, for instance, are usually much larger than humans. Thus, if you include small trees near *Apatosaurus*, the viewer will assume *Apatosaurus* is huge. Conversely, if you make the trees much larger than *Apatosaurus*, the dinosaur will appear smaller. And, if you draw a big flower towering over it, the viewer will see *Apatosaurus* as very tiny!

Tips on Color

Your picture will stand out from the rest of the crowd if you use these helpful tips on how to add color to your prehistoric masterpiece!

TRY WHITE ON BLACK

For a different look, try working on black construction or art paper. Then, instead of a pencil, you can use white chalk, white prismacolor pencil, or poster paint. With this technique, you'll need to concentrate on drawing the light areas in your picture rather than shadows.

TRY WHITE AND BLACK ON GRAY (OR TAN)

You don't need special gray or tan paper from the art store. Try cutting apart the inside of a grocery bag or a cereal box instead. This time, your background is a middle tone. Sketch your animal in black, then use white to make highlights. Add black for the shadows. Don't completely cover the tan or gray of the cardboard. Let it be the middle tone. With this technique, your pictures can have a very finished look with a minimal amount of drawing!

TRY COLOR

Instead of using every color in your marker set or your colored pencil set, try drawing in black for shadows, white for highlights, and one color for a middle tone. This third color blended with the white creates a fourth color. You will be surprised how professional your drawing will look.

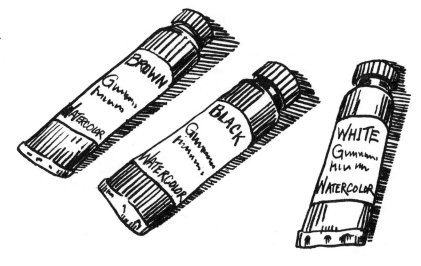